Friends' Journal

Friends' Journal

SHARED REFLECTIONS AND KEEPSAKES

Bluestreak
BOOKS

Bluestreak

Weldon Owen International
1045 Sansome Street, Suite 100, San Francisco, CA 94111
www.weldonowen.com

Library of Congress Cataloging in Publication data is available.

ISBN 978-1-68188-477-6

First Printed in 2019
10 9 8 7 6 5 4 3 2 1
2019 2020 2021 2022

Printed and bound in China

Illustration Credits:
Cover: © Shutterstock/ orangeberry
Interior: all art © Julia Dreams, except pages 30–31 © Tanya Syrytsyna

This book is dedicated to

_____

_____

_____

_____

Contents

How to use this book

Throughout this guided journal book, you'll find prompts that will help you explore your relationship as close friends, as well as your past, your present, and your future together. You and your friend will each complete your own profiles at the start of the book, with one of you choosing the I AM section and the other filling out the YOU ARE section. Throughout the rest of the journal, you'll each answer prompts depending on your profile. For some prompts, you'll want to brainstorm together with your friend and fill in what you've come up with. You can complete the book either by passing it back and forth, or by interviewing each other. The goal is to share and communicate with each other, and to record your thoughts, feelings, and memories together.

Some pages include blank areas in which you can add your own photographs using photo corners or other photo-safe scrapbooking supplies. If you don't have a photo, use the space to write a vivid description or sketch a picture of the moment. At the back of the book, you'll find an envelope where you can keep more photos, cards, notes, and other memories from your friendship, and preserve them for years to come.

INTRODUCTION

We are friends for life.
When we're together the years fall away.
Isn't that what matters? To have someone who
can remember with you? To have someone
who remembers how far you've come?

JUDY BLUME

Best Friends—is there a relationship more dependable, supportive, or more enriching? As best friends you share common interests, and fond, meaningful memories. You share ideas and tastes and often deep confidences, but you experience life as individuals. Sometimes you can get under each other's skin, yet you will always, hopefully, have each other's back. Your best friend feels your pain, and your joy too. You may know her like a family member, but she can still surprise you. You care about each other, argue with each other, protect each other, challenge each other. You can make each other cry, and you can make each other laugh till you cry.

Friendships are as unique as you each are individually. In these pages, explore your relationship—where you come from, how your relationship has evolved, and where you're going together. Your connection is strong and lifelong. Honor your bond here.

PART ONE

Who We Are

EXPLORING OUR
FRIENDSHIP

I AM . . .

*In the prompts throughout this book,
fill in the spaces labeled MY RESPONSE.*

My full name is _____

But you call me _____

_____

_____

I was born on _____

I am older than / younger than / same age as you

     (Circle one.)

Right now, I live _____

_____

_____

_____

_____

_____

_____

My memory of first meeting you

_____

_____

_____

_____

_____

_____

_____

_____

Here's a picture or keepsake from early in our relationship

YOU ARE . . .

*In the prompts throughout this book,
fill in the spaces labeled YOUR RESPONSE.*

My full name is _____

But you call me _____

_____

_____

I was born on _____

I am older than / younger than / same age as you

(Circle one.)

Right now, I live _____

_____

_____

_____

_____

_____

My memory of first meeting you _____

_____

_____

_____

_____

_____

_____

_____

Here's one of my favorite photos or keepsakes from early in our friendship

WE ARE . . .

Our relationship is

MY RESPONSE _____

_____

_____

_____

_____

YOUR RESPONSE _____

_____

_____

_____

_____

Describe yourself in one word.

MY RESPONSE _____

YOUR RESPONSE _____

Here are some words that describe your friend

MY RESPONSE _____

_____

_____

_____

_____

YOUR RESPONSE _____

_____

_____

_____

_____

Your friend's best qualities are

MY RESPONSE _____

_____

_____

_____

_____

YOUR RESPONSE _____

_____

_____

_____

Each of our parents or siblings might describe us as

MY RESPONSE _____

_____

_____

_____

YOUR RESPONSE _____

_____

_____

_____

Other people would describe us as

MY RESPONSE _____

_____

_____

_____

YOUR RESPONSE _____

_____

_____

_____

How are we similar?

MY RESPONSE _____

_____

_____

_____

_____

YOUR RESPONSE _____

_____

_____

_____

_____

How are we different?

MY RESPONSE _____

_____

_____

_____

_____

YOUR RESPONSE _____

_____

_____

_____

_____

One of my favorite memories from our time together is

MY RESPONSE _____

_____

_____

_____

_____

_____

_____

YOUR RESPONSE _____

_____

_____

_____

_____

_____

_____

_____

One of the times we laughed the hardest was

MY RESPONSE _____

_____

_____

YOUR RESPONSE _____

_____

_____

This is an event that sparked a running joke or ridiculous nickname that always makes us laugh

MY RESPONSE

Running joke or nickname _____

What happened _____

_____

_____

_____

_____

YOUR RESPONSE _____

Running joke or nickname _____

What happened _____

_____

_____

_____

> "Only a true best friend can protect you
> from your immortal enemies."
>
> RICHELLE MEAD, *VAMPIRE ACADEMY*

One of the most difficult times we've been through together was

MY RESPONSE _____

_____

YOUR RESPONSE _____

_____

This is something I had to do alone, but I always wish you could have been there with me

MY RESPONSE _____

_____

_____

_____

YOUR RESPONSE _____

_____

_____

_____

_____

The time in my life when I needed you the most was

MY RESPONSE _____

_____

_____

_____

_____

YOUR RESPONSE _____

_____

_____

_____

_____

And you were there for me by

MY RESPONSE _____

_____

_____

_____

_____

YOUR RESPONSE _____

_____

_____

_____

_____

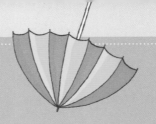

"Friends don't spy;
true friendship is about privacy, too."

STEPHEN KING

Shhh! This is a secret we kept between ourselves _____

MY RESPONSE _____

_____

_____

YOUR RESPONSE _____

_____

_____

_____

I need to come clean: This is something I may have said about you to other friends behind your back.

MY RESPONSE _____

_____

_____

_____

YOUR RESPONSE _____

_____

_____

_____

We may have been troublemakers together when

MY RESPONSE _____

_____

_____

YOUR RESPONSE _____

_____

_____

Were there any consequences?

MY RESPONSE _____

_____

_____

YOUR RESPONSE _____

_____

_____

This is one time I totally covered for you or had your back when you were in trouble.

MY RESPONSE _____

_____

_____

YOUR RESPONSE _____

_____

_____

"You only really fall apart in front of the people you know can piece you back together."

SARAH DESSEN, SAINT ANYTHING

When you're upset, you

MY RESPONSE _____

_____

_____

YOUR RESPONSE _____

_____

_____

I try to help by

MY RESPONSE _____

_____

_____

_____

YOUR RESPONSE _____

_____

_____

_____

Our biggest argument was over this issue

MY RESPONSE _____

_____

_____

_____

_____

YOUR RESPONSE _____

_____

_____

_____

_____

This is how we settled that argument, and what we learned from it

MY RESPONSE _____

_____

_____

_____

_____

YOUR RESPONSE _____

_____

_____

_____

The friends in a movie, book, or TV show who are most like us are

MY RESPONSE _____

_____

_____

_____

YOUR RESPONSE _____

_____

_____

_____

Because

MY RESPONSE _____

_____

_____

_____

_____

YOUR RESPONSE _____

_____

_____

_____

If our friendship was played out in a movie, it would be this genre

MY RESPONSE _____

because _____

_____

YOUR RESPONSE _____

because _____

_____

The actress who would play you would be

MY RESPONSE _____

because _____

_____

YOUR RESPONSE _____

because _____

_____

The actress who would play me would be

MY RESPONSE _____

because _____

_____

YOUR RESPONSE _____

because _____

_____

The movie's title would be

MY RESPONSE _____

YOUR RESPONSE _____

HOW WE CONNECT

"Which of all my important nothings
shall I tell you first?"

JANE AUSTEN

WE STAY IN TOUCH . . .

(Circle one for each row)

BY TEXTING	almost nonstop	at least once a day to see how you're doing	once in a while	I don't text
ON SOCIAL MEDIA	all the time, about everything	I look at your feed sometimes	I wouldn't know what you are up to without it	I deleted my account
BY PHONE	every day	every week	once in a while	just text me!

Other creative ways we do connect or could connect _____

_____

Do we talk to each other enough, not enough, or too much? _____

_____

If not enough How can we connect more? _____

_____

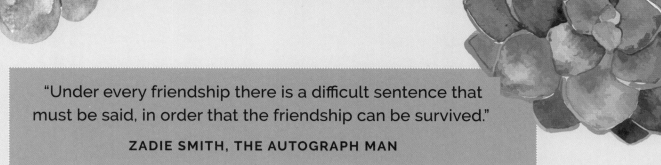

> "Under every friendship there is a difficult sentence that must be said, in order that the friendship can be survived."
>
> **ZADIE SMITH, THE AUTOGRAPH MAN**

The topics we talk about most are

MY RESPONSE _____

_____

_____

_____

YOUR RESPONSE _____

_____

_____

_____

The topics we don't love talking about are

MY RESPONSE _____

_____

_____

_____

_____

YOUR RESPONSE _____

_____

_____

_____

I always call you when I'm feeling

MY RESPONSE _____

_____

_____

YOUR RESPONSE _____

_____

_____

I'll never forget when I got this phone call from you

MY RESPONSE _____

_____

_____

_____

_____

YOUR RESPONSE _____

_____

_____

_____

The hardest conversation we've ever had was

MY RESPONSE _____

_____

_____

YOUR RESPONSE _____

_____

_____

_____

The most exciting conversations we've ever had were about

MY RESPONSE _____

_____

_____

_____

YOUR RESPONSE _____

_____

_____

_____

Add or describe a favorite piece of snail mail you've exchanged here, such as a greeting card, letter, note, or postcard

HANGING OUT

"It is more fun to talk with someone who doesn't use long, difficult words but rather short, easy words like, 'What about lunch?'"

A. A. MILNE, WINNIE-THE-POOH

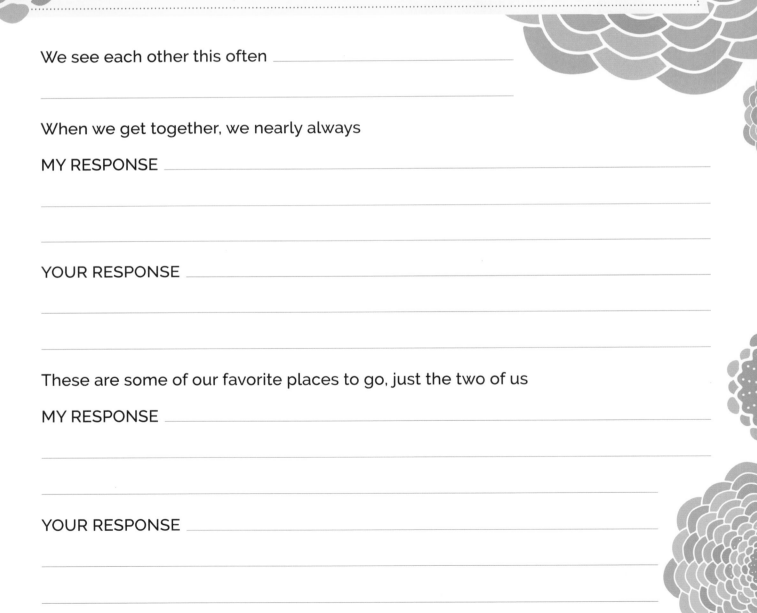

We see each other this often _____

_____

When we get together, we nearly always

MY RESPONSE _____

_____

_____

YOUR RESPONSE _____

_____

_____

These are some of our favorite places to go, just the two of us

MY RESPONSE _____

_____

_____

YOUR RESPONSE _____

_____

Our idea of a fun night hanging out together is

MY RESPONSE _____

_____

_____

_____

YOUR RESPONSE _____

_____

_____

_____

Something we used to do that we haven't done in a while is

MY RESPONSE _____

_____

_____

_____

YOUR RESPONSE _____

_____

_____

_____

My favorite thing to do with you is

MY RESPONSE _____

_____

_____

_____

YOUR RESPONSE _____

_____

_____

_____

A FEW OF OUR FAVORITE THINGS

Here are a few lists of what we love.

FASHION ACCESSORY

MY RESPONSE _____   YOUR RESPONSE _____

TIME OF YEAR

MY RESPONSE _____   YOUR RESPONSE _____

BOOKS

1. _____   1. _____

2. _____   2. _____

3. _____   3. _____

TV SHOWS OR YouTube VIDEOS

1. _____   1. _____

2. _____   2. _____

3. _____   3. _____

MOVIES

1. _____   1. _____

2. _____   2. _____

3. _____   3. _____

ACTORS & ACTRESSES

1. _____   1. _____

2. _____   2. _____

3. _____   3. _____

MUSIC BANDS

1. _____   1. _____

2. _____   2. _____

3. _____   3. _____

SONGS

1. _____   1. _____

2. _____   2. _____

3. _____   3. _____

GAMES

1. _____   1. _____

2. _____   2. _____

3. _____   3. _____

PLACES IN THE WORLD

1. _____   1. _____

2. _____   2. _____

3. _____   3. _____

GUILTY PLEASURES

**Here are some of our guilty pleasures.
Do *not* tell anyone!**

A totally terrible movie that I absolutely love is

MY RESPONSE _____

YOUR RESPONSE _____

I can't help but watch it, and you should too because

MY RESPONSE _____

_____

YOUR RESPONSE _____

_____

Please do not tell anyone that I binge-watched this TV show

MY RESPONSE _____

YOUR RESPONSE _____

I can't help but love it, and you should too because

MY RESPONSE _____

_____

YOUR RESPONSE _____

_____

A song that I'm embarrassed to know all the words to is

MY RESPONSE _____

YOUR RESPONSE _____

We sometime sang together to these tunes

1. _____

2. _____

3. _____

Online, I can't help but watch these YouTube videos

MY RESPONSE _____

YOUR RESPONSE _____

The star that I follow on social media that I hope no one can see in my follow list is

MY RESPONSE _____

_____

YOUR RESPONSE _____

_____

This is one more totally embarrassing thing that you know about me—and that no one else does (please keep it that way)

MY RESPONSE _____

_____

_____

YOUR RESPONSE _____

_____

_____

LET'S EAT

My three favorite dishes

MY RESPONSE

1. _____

2. _____

3. _____

YOUR RESPONSE

1. _____

2. _____

3. _____

I can't believe you don't like to eat

MY RESPONSE _____

_____

YOUR RESPONSE _____

_____

Our favorite restaurants are

1. _____

2. _____

3. _____

4. _____

5. _____

If I'm going to make you dinner, here's the recipe for something I'd make that I think you would *love*

MY RESPONSE

Ingredients _____

_____

_____

Instructions _____

_____

_____

_____

_____

_____

_____

YOUR RESPONSE

Ingredients _____

_____

_____

Instructions _____

_____

_____

_____

_____

_____

The home-cooked meal that I loved the most growing up and I most want to share with you

_____

Made by _____

_____

We usually ate it _____

_____

HERE'S THE RECIPE

Ingredients _____

_____

_____

_____

Instructions _____

_____

_____

_____

_____

_____

_____

_____

_____

_____

The home-cooked meal that I loved the most growing up and I most want to share with you

_____

Made by _____

_____

We usually ate it _____

_____

HERE'S THE RECIPE

Ingredients _____

_____

_____

_____

Instructions _____

_____

_____

_____

_____

_____

_____

_____

STYLE

"True friends are like diamonds—bright, beautiful, valuable, and always in style."

NICOLE RICHIE

I would describe your style as

MY RESPONSE _____

_____

YOUR RESPONSE _____

_____

My favorite outfit you wear is

MY RESPONSE _____

_____

YOUR RESPONSE _____

_____

My favorite piece of clothing you've leant me or given to me is

MY RESPONSE _____

_____

YOUR RESPONSE _____

_____

My favorite accessory you wear is

MY RESPONSE _____

_____

YOUR RESPONSE _____

_____

A style I think you should try is

MY RESPONSE _____

_____

YOUR RESPONSE _____

_____

We clean up nice! I remember how amazing you looked when you dressed up in this for a special occasion

MY RESPONSE _____

Event _____

Description of your friend _____

_____

YOUR RESPONSE _____

Event _____

Description of your friend _____

_____

OK. I never told you, but the most unflattering look you tried was

MY RESPONSE _____

_____

YOUR RESPONSE _____

THANK YOU

*"If you have two friends in your lifetime, you're lucky.
If you have one good friend, you're more than lucky."*

S.E. HINTON

Thank you for teaching me

MY RESPONSE _____

_____

_____

_____

_____

YOUR RESPONSE _____

_____

_____

_____

_____

Thank you for talking me out of

MY RESPONSE _____

_____

_____

YOUR RESPONSE _____

_____

_____

Thank you for saving the day when

MY RESPONSE _____

_____

_____

_____

YOUR RESPONSE _____

_____

_____

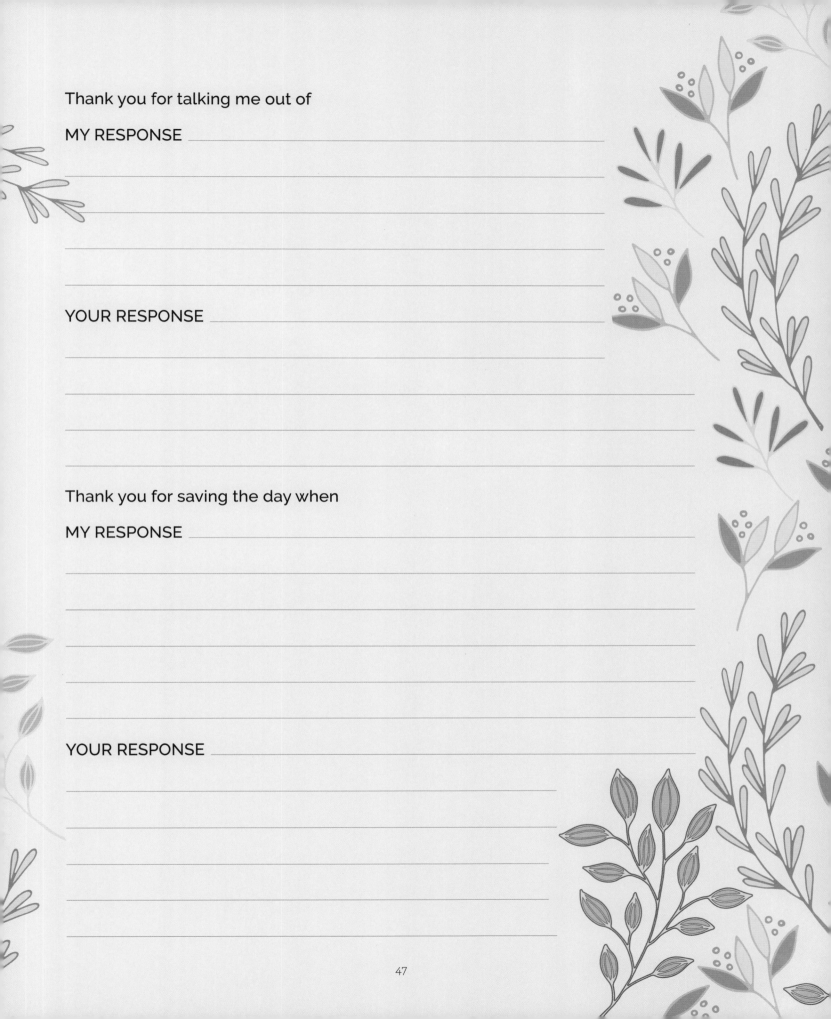

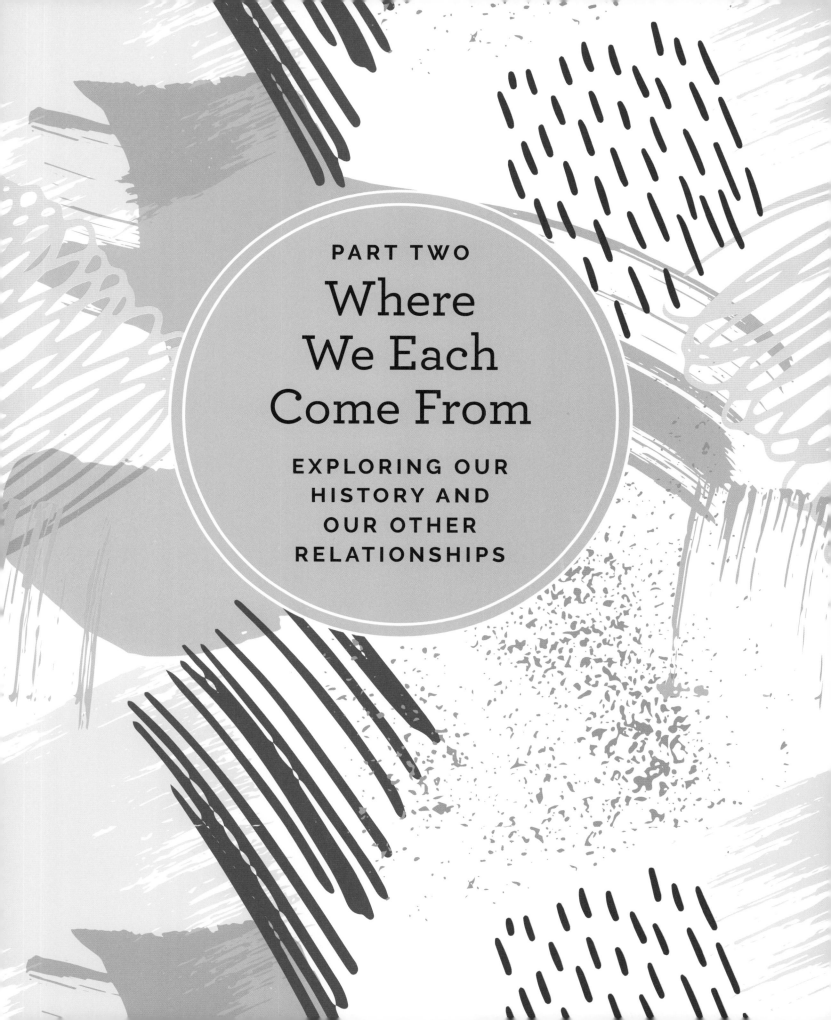

PART TWO

Where We Each Come From

EXPLORING OUR
HISTORY AND
OUR OTHER
RELATIONSHIPS

OUR SEPARATE FAMILIES

Family is the most important thing in the world.

PRINCESS DIANA

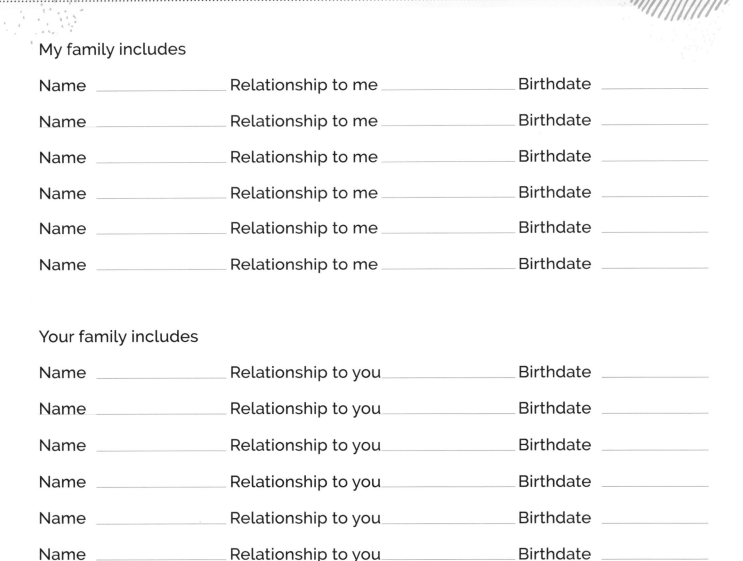

My family includes

Name _____ Relationship to me _____ Birthdate _____

Name _____ Relationship to me _____ Birthdate _____

Name _____ Relationship to me _____ Birthdate _____

Name _____ Relationship to me _____ Birthdate _____

Name _____ Relationship to me _____ Birthdate _____

Name _____ Relationship to me _____ Birthdate _____

Your family includes

Name _____ Relationship to you _____ Birthdate _____

Name _____ Relationship to you _____ Birthdate _____

Name _____ Relationship to you _____ Birthdate _____

Name _____ Relationship to you _____ Birthdate _____

Name _____ Relationship to you _____ Birthdate _____

Name _____ Relationship to you _____ Birthdate _____

My relationship to my family is like _____

_____

MY MOST LOVING AND SUPPORTIVE MEMORIES _____

_____

_____

MY FAMILY CAN BE MOST CHALLENGING WHEN _____

_____

_____

Your relationship to your family is like _____

_____

YOUR MOST LOVING AND SUPPORTIVE MEMORIES _____

_____

_____

_____

YOUR FAMILY CAN BE MOST CHALLENGING WHEN _____

_____

_____

Your favorite thoughts about my family _____

_____

My favorite thoughts about your family _____

_____

_____

Add photos of or describe a favorite memory we've had with each other's families

Add a photo of or describe a fun gathering.

These are the good qualities I learned from my family, and who most inspired me

MY RESPONSE

1. Quality _____ Who I get it from _____

2. Quality _____ Who I get it from _____

3. Quality _____ Who I get it from _____

These are the good qualities you learned from your family, and who most inspired you

YOUR RESPONSE

1. Quality _____ Who you get it from _____

2. Quality _____ Who you get it from _____

3. Quality _____ Who you get it from _____

These are some bad qualities I might have picked up from my family, and who was most responsible

1. Quality _____ Who I get it from _____

2. Quality _____ Who I get it from _____

3. Quality _____ Who I get it from _____

These are some bad qualities you might have picked up from your family, and who was most responsible

1. Quality _____ Who you get it from _____

2. Quality _____ Who you get it from _____

3. Quality _____ Who you get it from _____

OTHER CLOSE PEOPLE IN OUR EXTENDED LIVES

GRANDPARENTS, AUNTS AND UNCLES,
COUSINS, FAMILY FRIENDS, TEACHERS AND
SCHOOL FRIENDS INSPIRE US.
HERE ARE SOME PEOPLE IN OUR EXTENDED WORLD
WHO WE ADMIRE AND WHO HAVE INSPIRED US.

Name _____

Who they are to us _____

_____

Describe their relationship to us in a few words

MY RESPONSE _____

YOUR RESPONSE _____

What we learned from them

MY RESPONSE _____

_____

YOUR RESPONSE _____

_____

Name _____

Who they are to us _____

_____

Describe their relationship to us in a few words

MY RESPONSE _____

YOUR RESPONSE _____

What we learned from them

MY RESPONSE _____

_____

YOUR RESPONSE

_____

_____

Name _____

Who they are to us _____

_____

Describe their relationship to us in a few words

MY RESPONSE _____

YOUR RESPONSE _____

What we learned from them

MY RESPONSE _____

_____

YOUR RESPONSE _____

_____

INSPIRATIONAL PEOPLE

PUBLIC FIGURES OR INSPIRING LITERARY OR HISTORICAL FIGURES

Name _____

Describe this individual in three words _____

Why this person is important to us _____

_____

_____

_____

Name _____

Describe this individual in three words _____

Why this person is important to us _____

_____

_____

_____

Name _____

Describe this individual in three words _____

Why this person is important to us _____

_____

_____

_____

Name _____

Describe this individual in three words _____

Why this person is important to us _____

_____

_____

_____

Name _____

Describe this individual in three words _____

Why this person is important to us _____

_____

_____

_____

Name _____

Describe this individual in three words _____

Why this person is important to us _____

_____

_____

INSPIRATIONAL MOMENTS IN OUR LIVES

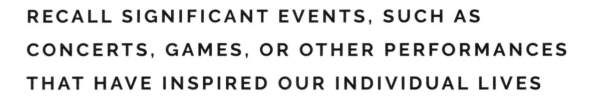

RECALL SIGNIFICANT EVENTS, SUCH AS CONCERTS, GAMES, OR OTHER PERFORMANCES THAT HAVE INSPIRED OUR INDIVIDUAL LIVES

Describe this event _____

_____

_____

Why this event was important to one or both of us _____

_____

_____

_____

_____

_____

_____

Describe this event _____

_____

_____

_____

Why this event was important to one or both of us _____

_____

_____

_____

_____

_____

_____

_____

Describe this event _____

_____

_____

_____

Why this event was important to one or both of us _____

_____

_____

_____

_____

_____

_____

TRADITIONS

TRADITIONS ARE THE RITUALS WE CARRY ON
THROUGH GENERATIONS. THEY CAN BE RELIGIOUS
OR CULTURAL, THEY CAN MARK SPECIAL OCCASIONS,
OR THEY CAN EVEN BE SMALL, EVERYDAY GESTURES
THAT FAMILY MEMBERS DO FOR EACH OTHER. EXPLORE
YOUR INDIVIDUAL FAMILY TRADITIONS, OLD AND NEW,
OR WHAT YOU EACH MAY WANT TO CARRY FORWARD,
AND WHAT YOU MIGHT LEAVE BEHIND.

These are some of the traditions my family takes part in

_____

_____

These are some of the traditions your family takes part in _____

_____

_____

We use these traditions to remember loved ones we've lost

MY RESPONSE _____

_____

YOUR RESPONSE _____

_____

These are the traditions I plan to carry forward with my family and future generations

MY RESPONSE _____

_____

YOUR RESPONSE _____

_____

I probably won't continue these traditions

MY RESPONSE _____

_____

YOUR RESPONSE _____

_____

Add a photo that shows your family taking part in an important tradition.

WHERE WE GREW UP

We spent most of our childhood at these addresses

MY RESPONSE _____

YOUR RESPONSE _____

Describe your childhood home

MY RESPONSE _____

_____

YOUR RESPONSE _____

_____

Describe your hometown

MY RESPONSE _____

_____

_____

YOUR RESPONSE _____

_____

_____

_____

These are some places we each loved to visit when we were growing up—parks, beaches, museums, and more

MY RESPONSE _____

_____

_____

YOUR RESPONSE _____

_____

_____

These are places we each traveled to often—like relatives' houses, favorite vacation spots, and summer camps we returned to again and again

MY RESPONSE _____

_____

_____

_____

YOUR RESPONSE _____

_____

_____

These are other important places in our story as friends—places we like to go to together.

MY RESPONSE _____

_____

_____

YOUR RESPONSE _____

_____

_____

MEMORIES FROM OUR CHILDHOOD

WHAT WERE WE LIKE AS KIDS? WHAT WERE SOME OF THE INTERESTS WE MAY HAVE SHARED IF WE HAD KNOWN EACH OTHER BACK THEN?

These are some of the things we did to entertain ourselves when we were kids

MY RESPONSE _____

_____

_____

YOUR RESPONSE _____

_____

_____

These are some of the imaginary roles we took on when we were playing

MY RESPONSE _____

_____

_____

YOUR RESPONSE _____

_____

_____

Sometimes we got these people involved in our games

MY RESPONSE _____

_____

YOUR RESPONSE _____

_____

Describe one of the games that you still remember now, in detail

MY RESPONSE _____

_____

_____

_____

_____

YOUR RESPONSE _____

_____

_____

_____

_____

Add photos of each of you as children

SHARED JOY

SOME OF THE HAPPIEST MOMENTS IN LIFE HAPPEN DURING BIRTHDAYS, HOLIDAYS, AND OTHER SPECIAL OCCASIONS. REMEMBER SOME OF THE HAPPY MOMENTS YOU SHARED.

Here's a memory from one of your birthdays that I'll always remember

MY RESPONSE

You were turning _____ I was this old _____

This is what I remember _____

_____

_____

YOUR RESPONSE

You were turning _____ I was this old _____

This is what I remember _____

_____

_____

The best birthday present you ever gave me was

MY RESPONSE

Gift _____

Why I love it so much _____

_____

_____

YOUR RESPONSE

Gift _____

Why I love it so much _____

_____

_____

My favorite memory from an event we attended together was

MY RESPONSE _____

Event/Celebration _____ Year _____

My memory is _____

_____

_____

_____

YOUR RESPONSE _____

Event/Celebration _____ Year _____

My memory is _____

_____

_____

_____

This was a truly memorable vacation

MY RESPONSE _____

Where we went _____

Who else was there _____

Some things we did during that vacation were _____

_____

_____

A memory from that vacation is _____

_____

_____

_____

_____

YOUR RESPONSE

Where we went _____

Who else was there _____

Some things we did during that vacation are _____

_____

A memory from that vacation is _____

_____

_____

_____

Add a photo from or describe another vacation we took together

IMPORTANT MOMENTS

EVENTS SHAPE US AND OUR RELATIONSHIPS, ESPECIALLY BIG LIFE EVENTS LIKE BIRTHS, DEATHS, MARRIAGES, AND MORE. HERE ARE MOMENTOUS OCCASIONS WE'VE EXPERIENCED TOGETHER

Important event _____

Date _____

The event was for this person or these people _____

_____

This moment was important because

MY RESPONSE _____

YOUR RESPONSE _____

A memory I have about you from this event is

MY RESPONSE _____

_____

YOUR RESPONSE _____

_____

Important event _____

Date _____

The event was for this person or these people _____

_____

This moment was important because

MY RESPONSE _____

_____

_____

_____

YOUR RESPONSE _____

_____

_____

_____

A memory I have from this event is

MY RESPONSE _____

_____

_____

_____

_____

YOUR RESPONSE _____

_____

_____

_____

_____

ACCOMPLISHMENTS

I was really proud of you when you accomplished

MY RESPONSE _____

_____

_____

_____

YOUR RESPONSE _____

_____

_____

_____

You were proud of me when I accomplished

MY RESPONSE _____

_____

_____

YOUR RESPONSE _____

_____

_____

Another time I was really happy for you was when you

MY RESPONSE _____

_____

_____

_____

_____

YOUR RESPONSE _____

_____

_____

_____

_____

Because

MY RESPONSE _____

_____

_____

_____

YOUR RESPONSE _____

_____

_____

PART THREE

Looking Ahead Together

ON THE HORIZON

"I am treating you as my friend,
asking you to share my present minuses in the hope
that I can ask you to share my future plusses."

KATHERINE MANSFIELD

In the near or distant future, these are some important events coming up in our lives

MY RESPONSE

What's on my horizon _____

_____

How you'll be there for me _____

_____

_____

What's on my horizon _____

_____

How you'll be there for me _____

_____

_____

What's on my horizon _____

_____

How you'll be there for me _____

_____

YOUR RESPONSE

What's on my horizon _____

_____

_____

How you'll be there for me _____

_____

_____

_____

What's on my horizon _____

_____

_____

How you'll be there for me _____

_____

_____

_____

What's on my horizon _____

_____

_____

How you'll be there for me _____

_____

_____

When I think about my future, I'm worried or anxious about these moments, and here's how I'll need your support

MY RESPONSE

What's on my horizon _____

_____

How you can support me _____

_____

_____

_____

What's on my horizon _____

_____

How you can support me _____

_____

_____

_____

What's on my horizon _____

_____

How you can support me _____

_____

_____

_____

YOUR RESPONSE

What's on my horizon _____

_____

How you can support me _____

_____

_____

_____

_____

What's on my horizon _____

_____

How you can support me _____

_____

_____

_____

What's on my horizon _____

_____

How you can support me _____

_____

_____

_____

MAKING PLANS

If we could go on three perfect friendship outings, they would be

MY RESPONSE

1. _____

_____

2. _____

_____

3. _____

_____

YOUR RESPONSE

1. _____

_____

2. _____

_____

3. _____

_____

This is one of my favorite things we've done together, and I'd like to do it again

MY RESPONSE

What we did _____

_____

Why we should do it again _____

_____

_____

_____

YOUR RESPONSE

What we did _____

_____

Why we should do it again _____

_____

_____

_____

Add a photo of or describe another favorite activity that you did together

Here's a place I'd like to travel to with you

MY RESPONSE _____

Place _____

This is why _____

_____

_____

These are some of the things we could do there together _____

_____

_____

_____

_____

YOUR RESPONSE

Place _____

This is why _____

_____

_____

These are some of the things we could do there together _____

_____

_____

_____

_____

OUR FRIENDSHIP BUCKET LIST

HERE'S EVERYTHING WE HAVEN'T DONE YET, BUT WE WANT TO DO TOGETHER—NOW, SOON, OR IN THE FUTURE

- ☐ _____
- ☐ _____
- ☐ _____
- ☐ _____
- ☐ _____
- ☐ _____
- ☐ _____
- ☐ _____
- ☐ _____
- ☐ _____
- ☐ _____
- ☐ _____
- ☐ _____
- ☐ _____

YOU CAN DO THIS!
CHALLENGE EACH OTHER TO DO SOMETHING THAT MIGHT BE AMBITIOUS OR PHYSICALLY CHALLENGING BUT COULD BE LIFE-CHANGING!

I dare you to _____

_____

_____

YOUR RESPONSE _____

_____

_____

Challenge accepted? ☐ Yes! ☐ No way!

You dare me to _____

_____

_____

MY RESPONSE _____

_____

_____

Challenge accepted? ☐ Yes! ☐ No way!

Double-dare! We dare *ourselves* to do this together _____

_____

_____

_____

This was one time we went outside of our comfort zone together—and loved it!

Here's what we did _____

_____

_____

_____

_____

_____

_____

_____

_____

_____

_____

_____

_____

_____

_____

_____

_____

TO COMPLETE THE FOLLOWING PAGES, TALK TO YOUR FRIENDS AND FAMILY AND BRAINSTORM SOME IDEAS TOGETHER

The future is full of potential for creating new memories with your loved ones.

Think about what you can make happen by using your friendship powers!

New traditions, anniversary events, trips of a lifetime to honor your heritage,

or a simple dinner party featuring your family's favorite dishes—these are some

activities you can do to create new memories with the important people in your life.

ACTIVITIES WE COULD DO, NEAR OR FAR

Activity _____

_____

_____

People we'd like to join us _____

Activity _____

_____

_____

People we'd like to join us _____

Activity _____

_____

_____

People we'd like to join us _____

FRIENDS, UNITE!

IS THERE A PROJECT YOU'VE ALWAYS WANTED TO TACKLE TOGETHER? A CAUSE THAT'S NEAR AND DEAR TO YOUR HEARTS? ARE THERE IMPORTANT PEOPLE IN YOUR LIVES THAT YOU WANT TO HONOR, TOGETHER? HERE ARE SOME WAYS WE CAN WORK TOGETHER FOR OTHERS

A project we've always talked about doing together is _____

_____

This feels important or exciting to us because _____

_____

_____

Here's what we need to do to make this project a reality _____

_____

_____

A cause that we care about is _____

_____

_____

Here are a few ideas for how we can get involved together _____

_____

_____

These are people who have helped shape our lives as friends—parents, grandparents, siblings, other relatives, neighbors, friends—and some ideas for things we can do together to celebrate or honor them

Person _____

What we could do _____

_____

Person _____

What we could do _____

_____

Person _____

What we could do _____

_____

Person _____

What we could do _____

_____

Person _____

What we could do _____

_____

Person _____

What we could do _____

_____

Person _____

What we could do _____

_____

> "Friendship is a give and take. You have to have a strong relationship with your friend and I think you have to offer them something and they have to offer you something and that's to always learn from it."

RAVEN SYMONE

LOOKING BACK ON OUR STORY
PAGE BACK THROUGH THE RESPONSES YOU'VE WRITTEN IN THIS BOOK BEFORE ANSWERING THESE QUESTIONS.

What is the most surprising thing you've learned about your friend in these pages?

MY RESPONSE _____

_____

YOUR RESPONSE _____

_____

Is there something your friend wrote about you here that surprised you?
If so, how did that make you feel?

MY RESPONSE _____

_____

YOUR RESPONSE _____

_____

Is there something new that you learned about how you relate to your friend?

MY RESPONSE _____

_____

YOUR RESPONSE _____

_____

_____

HOPES AND THOUGHTS
FOR THE FUTURE

My hopes for you are

MY RESPONSE _____

_____

_____

_____

_____

_____

_____

_____

_____

_____

_____

_____

YOUR RESPONSE

My hopes for us are

MY RESPONSE

YOUR RESPONSE

If you're ever feeling unsure about yourself, remember this about who you are

MY RESPONSE _____

_____

_____

_____

_____

_____

_____

YOUR RESPONSE _____

_____

_____

_____

_____

_____

_____

_____

These are all the reasons why I feel so lucky to have you as my friend

MY RESPONSE _____

_____

_____

_____

_____

_____

_____

_____

YOUR RESPONSE _____

_____

_____

_____

_____

_____

_____

_____

_____

OUR FAVORITE PHOTOS OF US TOGETHER

MY RESPONSE

This is my favorite photo of us. It was taken in _____ at _____
(year)   *(place)*

I love it because _____

_____

YOUR RESPONSE

This is my favorite photo of us. It was taken in _____ at _____
(year)   *(place)*

I love it because _____

_____